Low Fat
slim, healthy, and full of vitality
makes you fit

**LESS FAT IN YOUR DIET
MORE POWER IN YOUR
EVERYDAY LIFE**

Having enough energy for the job, staying slim, yet not going hungry, that is the secret of Low Fat. Many people lack active elements in the form of vitamins, minerals, and carbohydrates. The culprit is the excessive amount of fatty foods on our plates. If you are often tired and unable to concentrate, or you find you are sinking under the stress of your job, it can be a sign that there are not enough healthy, fitness-promoting foods in your diet. And with one in three people now being overweight and taking insufficient exercise, Low Fat is more important than ever. Low-fat dishes contain a maximum of 30 per cent of the daily calorie intake in the form of fat. The remaining 70 per cent of the calories provide protein and carbohydrate, as recommended by nutrition experts. This proportion is perfect for your weight and your health. People who are overweight and who try to follow the 30 per cent low-fat rule will, over a period of time, automatically lose several pounds, and that's without even dieting or going hungry.

CARBOHYDRATES FOR INCREASED VITALITY

Fatty calories account for a good 40 per cent of our daily food intake, which means that carbohydrates are usually in short supply. For that reason, a low-fat diet contains plenty of carbohydrate, such as potatoes, bread, pasta, and rice. If you go for the wholemeal option, the positive effects of a low-fat diet will be more long lasting. As a result of the roughage hidden within in the wholemeal, the carbohydrates are absorbed into the blood more slowly, which means the invigorating effects of the carbohydrates last even longer. What's more, roughage is a natural way to activate sluggish bowels, as it reacts with the lactic acid bacteria in yogurt and buttermilk. Anyone who spends most of the time sitting and doesn't take much exercise should at least use diet to help get their bowels moving.

TIPS FOR LOW-FAT COOKING

If you watch out for a low-fat content both when choosing and when cooking food, you will automatically ensure that you have sufficient vital substances. But it is not advisable to do without fat altogether, as the body actually needs some fatty acids, primarily those contained in vegetable oils and in fish, for example.

Here are a few tips to help you use less fat when cooking:

Roast meat in very hot fat. This closes the pores, preventing them from absorbing any fat. Meat cooked in an earthenware dish or roasting bag requires no fat at all.

Steam your vegetables and fish in a steamer. This preserves the vital substances, and doesn't use a drop of fat.

Soften your vegetables or fish in water instead of oil or butter. Brush meat with oil before sautéing and cook in the hot frying pan without any fat. If you use a non-stick frying pan, you do not need to use any fat at all.

Deep-frying has no place in low-fat cooking, because practically any food cooked in a deep-fat fryer is guaranteed to make you fatter. There is some consolation for chip fans, though: frozen chips can be cooked in the oven without fat.

Grilling also requires no fat. It is best to place the meat on a sheet of aluminium foil on the grill without adding any fat.

Salad dressings: replace half the oil with vegetable stock, and combine thoroughly. Use an aromatic, cold pressed oil, to produce a fuller flavour with less oil.

Spread butter or margarine thinly on bread or rolls, or replace it entirely with low-fat crème fraîche for sweet toppings or tomato purée for savoury ones.

Eating at

Tempting alternatives to fast food

work

QUICK AND FULL OF VITAL SUBSTANCES

If your employer provides facilities for you to heat up food you have brought from home, then take advantage of this opportunity and enjoy your home-made fitness food at work.

The evening before, prepare your meal for the following day. Whether it's a favourite dish or a quick healthy snack, a packed lunch to be eaten cold, or a hot meal, you choose the dish you want. All you need are the right recipes. In the recipe section you will find plenty of suggestions for your working day. The dishes provide variety and are full of active substances. And all the ingredients can be found in any supermarket. That way, you have the double benefit of saving time and knowing exactly what you are eating.

Pack your working lunch in leak-proof plastic containers with tight-fitting lids. A huge range of non-breakable plastic containers is now available. You can choose from the various shapes, colours, and sizes available in a well-stocked kitchen shop or in the appropriate sections of department stores.

FITNESS FOOD ALL DAY LONG

Of course, no fitness diet starts just at lunchtime. If you want to retain or increase your vitality, there is a lot you can do, starting with breakfast. In the "Perfect Starters" chapter you will find just what you need to start your day. From page 44, you will find suggestions for hot suppertime treats. Those with a sweet tooth will also find something to their liking in the fruity desserts section. If you cannot heat up your own food at work, then simply swap the hot lunch for the evening meal.

Eating low fat does not mean that you have to lose out on taste. With the right combination of ingredients, you can enjoy wonderful flavours while still using very little fat. Experiment with lots of herbs such as basil, thyme, rosemary, chives, or parsley, and spices, such as nutmeg, curry powder, mustard, and pepper. Be more adventurous and try something new more often, and buy lots of fresh and low-fat foods. That way, you'll have only 30 per cent of the fat, but 100 per cent of the flavour.

Problem: Lunch break

If you cannot make something for yourself at work, it doesn't mean you have to resort to the fast food restaurant. Just choose dishes that don't need to be reheated, such as sandwiches or salads. And if every now and again you do go to the restaurant with your colleagues, there's no reason why you should look the odd-one-out ordering a low-fat meal. After all, many restaurants now include low-fat alternatives in their menus, and your canteen is sure to be no exception. With these tips, it is easy to follow the low-fat rule – maximum 30 per cent fat – and still enjoy your meal.

✽ Ask for a salad without any dressing and add the oil and vinegar yourself. That way you can choose the amount of oil you wish to add.

✽ Choose a clear soup instead of a rich, and highly calorific, cream soup.

✽ The main course should comprise fresh vegetables, fish or seafood, and rice or potatoes.

✽ Go easy on the sauce.

✽ You're sure to be on the right track if you give cheese gratin dishes a miss.

✽ For dessert, opt for fruit salads, jellies, or other puddings with plenty of fruit.

Low Fat

for increased vitality and a new zest for life

for every occasion

The recipes in this book are not just for people who complain they are a couple of pounds overweight, but also for people who watch what they eat and would like to focus on revitalizing their body. The table classifies the recipes from this book according to their Low Fat strengths. All of them are an unadulterated source of vital substances for fitness and to get your metabolism going at its best as and when required.

* Some dishes are just brim-full of minerals to give you energy and stamina, especially in the gym and when doing sport.

* Others contain not only fewer, but also healthier fats, and are also rich in vitamins to keep the heart and circulation young.

* Other dishes are a particularly rich source of specific vital substances that are perfect for people who are prone to 'flu because their immune system gets insufficient powerful resistance-strengthening substances.

* For vegetarians, the last column of the table contains original non-meat and non-fish recipes. No breakfast or dessert suggestions are listed here.

PLENTY OF MINERALS FOR FITNESS FANS

Honey-sweet sunrise
Rise and shine fruit rolls
Two-minute breakfast
Classic flake muesli
Tomato rolls with radishes
Marinated vegetables
Rocket salad with melon
Tex-Mex salad with kidney beans
Fruity kohlrabi salad
Turkey salad with chicory
Quick chilled tomato soup
Fennel and orange salad
Sweet fruit rolls
Sweet-and-savoury wholemeal sandwich
Spicy vegetable shake
Banana power drink
Vegetable casserole with pork
Celery and orange rice
Vegetable rice with Parmesan
Courgette and chicken soup
Fruit jelly
Sweet millet risotto with mango
Grape and cream cheese soufflé
Polenta fruit loaf with vanilla sauce

HEALTHY FATS & VITAMINS FOR HEART AND CIRCULATION

Yogurt and berry flakes

Two-minute breakfast

Classic flake muesli

Apple and mango muesli

Marinated vegetables

Tex-Mex salad with kidney beans

Fruity kohlrabi salad

Turkey salad with chicory

Quick chilled tomato soup

Fennel and orange salad

Bean sprout sandwich with cheese

Spicy vegetable shake

White cabbage and cod parcels

Tuna and pasta bake

Vegetable casserole with pork

Vegetable rice with Parmesan

Courgette and chicken soup

Pasta with prawns

Oriental stir-fry with pork fillet

Lambs' lettuce with trout fillet

Fruit jelly

Polenta fruit loaf with vanilla sauce

VITAL SUBSTANCES FOR INCREASED RESISTANCE

Melon with orange

Rise and shine fruit rolls

Two-minute breakfast

Tomato rolls with radishes

Apple and mango muesli

Marinated vegetables

Fruity kohlrabi salad

Turkey salad with chicory

Sauerkraut with pineapple

Fennel and orange salad

Sweet-and-savoury wholemeal sandwich

Spicy vegetable shake

Banana power drink

White cabbage and cod parcels

Fillet steak with broccoli rice

Vegetable casserole with pork

Vegetable rice with Parmesan

Fennel gratin

Lambs' lettuce with trout fillet

Polenta pizza with green pepper

Fruit jelly

Sweet millet risotto with mango

VEGETARIAN SNACKS AND MAIN DISHES

Marinated vegetables

Rocket salad with melon

Italian spaghetti salad

Tex-Mex salad with kidney beans

Fruity kohlrabi salad

Sauerkraut with pineapple

Quick chilled tomato soup

Fennel and orange salad

Fruity cheese sandwich

Sweet fruit rolls

Bean sprout sandwich with cheese

Red-and-green baguettes

Spicy vegetable shake

Pear and buttermilk flip

Banana power drink

Celery and orange rice

Potatoes with bean sprout cream

Potato and celeriac bake

Vegetable rice with Parmesan

Tomato and mozzarella boats

Polenta pizza with green pepper

Power

feast yourself fit

week

FIT NOT FAT

These low-fat recipes are the healthy way to lose pounds, as they will give you exactly the right combination of nutrients that your metabolism needs: not a drop of fat too much, and sufficient carbohydrate, so you will want for nothing. You won't experience any pangs of hunger, and you will enjoy increased vitality. Convert this unaccustomed energy into more exercise and sport. That way, you will lose even more weight and get your metabolism going for the long term.

THE PLAN FOR THE WEEK:
LOSE 1 KILOGRAM (2.2 LBS)
IN 7 DAYS

Eat well and lose weight at the same time, that's everybody's dream. But with the recipes contained in the following chapters, it really works. You can easily swap the midday meal for the evening meal. Each recipe is designed so that on average you eat only about 30 g (1 oz) of fat per day. Experience shows that, as a result, you will then lose about 1 kilogram (2.2 lbs) per week, even more if you have retained a lot of water.

REMEMBER:
DRINK PLENTY

Although the plan for the week includes no drink suggestions, it is extremely important to drink when you are trying to lose weight, even if you are not thirsty. Drink at least 1.5 litres (3 pints) per day, or better still, 2 litres (4 pints), to flush out any metabolic toxins that may occur while slimming. Mineral water, fruit or vegetable juices diluted with water, or even herbal teas are particularly good, as they are a source of vital substances.

EAT LOW-FAT SNACKS TO
COMBAT STRESS

If you are often working under pressure, you should allow yourself little snacks throughout the day. Some fruit, a few slices of sweet pepper or kohlrabi, some radishes, or rice biscuits will assuage the pangs of hunger and keep you fit, without a single extra gram of fat jeopardizing the success of your attempts to lose weight. You can also eat a low-fat yogurt, a low-fat fruit fromage frais, or a fruit juice to raise your spirits.

PLAN FOR THE WEEK

Monday

* Yogurt and berry flakes
* Tuna and pasta bake
* Red-and-green baguettes

Tuesday

* Classic flake muesli, with Pear and buttermilk flip
* Tomato and mozzarella boats
* Courgette and chicken soup

Wednesday

* Tomato rolls with radishes
* Grape and quark soufflé * Between-meals snack: Fruity kohlrabi salad
* Marinated vegetables

Thursday

* Honey-sweet sunrise
* Beef with mushrooms
* Rocket salad with melon * Fruit jelly

Friday

* Sweet fruit rolls
* Quick chilled tomato soup
* Pasta with prawns

Saturday

* Banana power drink
* Tex-Mex salad with kidney beans
* Potato and celeriac bake * Peach gratin

Sunday

* Apple and mango muesli
* Bean sprout sandwich with cheese * Between-meals snack: Spicy vegetable shake
* White cabbage and cod parcels

Melon

enough vitamin C

with

for the whole day

orange

Serves 2: • 1 small sweet melon • 2 pears • 2 oranges • 1 pot low-fat yogurt
(1.5% fat) • 1 tsp honey • ground cinnamon

Cut the melon in half horizontally and use a spoon to remove the seeds.
Halve, peel, and core the pears, then chop up small. Peel the oranges,
removing all the white pith. Remove the fruit from the orange segments,
passing a small paring knife between the flesh and the membranes.
Combine with the yogurt and pear pieces. Add the honey and cinnamon to
taste. Spoon the mixture into the melon halves. Serve with a sprinkling of
cinnamon (optional).

power

PER PORTION: 302 KCAL • 6 G PROTEIN • 2 G FAT • 65 G CARBOHYDRATE

Rise and shine

The quick energy boost

fruit rolls

Serves 2: • 3 wholemeal bread rolls • 3 tbsp low-fat cream cheese • 1 banana • 2 kiwi fruit • 1 vanilla pod • Icing sugar (optional)

Cut the bread rolls in half and spread the cream cheese thinly over each half. Peel the banana and kiwi fruit, cut a few slices of each, and set aside. Purée the remaining fruit. Slit the vanilla pod open lengthways, scrape out the seeds inside, and add them to the fruit purée. Add icing sugar to taste. Spread the purée over the bread roll halves, and garnish with the remaining fruit slices.

PER PORTION: 257 KCAL • 9 G PROTEIN • 3 G FAT • 70 G CARBOHYDRATE

Two-minute

the fruity drink to make you fit

breakfast

Serves 2: • 200 ml (7 fl oz) orange juice • 100 ml (3 1/2 fl oz) naturally cloudy apple juice • 100 ml (3 1/2 fl oz) blackcurrant juice • 1 tbsp oat bran flakes • honey • 2 tbsp berries of your choice

Combine the orange, apple, and blackcurrant juices with the oat bran flakes. Sweeten to taste with a little honey. Wash and hull the berries, cutting larger berries into halves or quarters. Pour into 2 glasses, garnish with the berries, and serve.

PER PORTION: 115 KCAL • 2 G PROTEIN • 1 G FAT • 23 G CARBOHYDRATE

Yogurt and berry flakes

a fortifying start to the day

Serves 2: • 100 g (4 oz) berries, mixed or seasonal • 200 g (7 oz) low-fat yogurt (1.5% fat) • honey to taste • 80 g (3 oz) cornflakes

Wash and hull the berries, cutting any larger ones into halves or quarters, and setting a few aside for decoration. Coarsely crush the remaining berries with a fork, combine with the yogurt in a bowl, and, if necessary, sweeten with the honey, depending on the sweetness of the berries. Fold the cornflakes into the berry and yogurt mixture, and decorate with the remaining berries.

PER PORTION: 246 KCAL • 6 G PROTEIN • 2 G FAT • 52 G CARBOHYDRATE

Honey-sweet

with melon balls and orange segments

sunrise

Serves 2: • 1/2 sweet melon • 2 oranges • 80 g (3 oz) cornflakes • 100 ml (3 1/2 fl oz) orange juice • 1 pot low-fat yogurt (1.5% fat) • honey to taste • berries for decoration

Remove the seeds from the melon half. Use a melon scoop to make small balls from the flesh. Peel the oranges, removing all the white pith. Remove the fruit from the orange segments, passing a small paring knife between the flesh and the membranes. Mix the melon balls and cornflakes together. Stir in the orange juice and yogurt and add honey to taste. Wash the berries and scatter them on top.

PER PORTION: 338 KCAL • 8 G PROTEIN • 2 G FAT • 71 G CARBOHYDRATE

Classic flake

the time-tested fitness combination

muesli

Serves 2:

10 tbsp grain flakes, mixed

1 tbsp oat flakes

400 ml (14 fl oz) low-fat milk (1.5% fat)

2 bananas

2 large apples

4 tbsp raisins

honey

1 orange

Stir the grain and oat flakes into the milk. Peel the bananas. Cut half of one banana into slices, then coarsely crush the remaining bananas with a fork. Thoroughly wash and dry the apples, then grate them coarsely, with the skin on, but excluding the core. Immediately stir the grated apple and the banana purée into the flake muesli. Add the raisins and sweeten to taste with honey.

Peel the orange, removing all the white pith. Remove the fruit from the orange segments, passing a small paring knife between the flesh and the membranes. Decorate the muesli as you like with the orange segments and banana slices, and serve immediately.

Muesli to go

You can take flake muesli with you to work for a mid-morning snack. Just mix the flakes with the grated apple, orange segments, raisins, and honey, and put in a container. Blend the banana with the milk, transfer to a plastic bottle with a tight-fitting lid, and stir into the flake mixture when it's time for elevenses.

power

PER PORTION: 407 KCAL

11 G PROTEIN • 5 G FAT

86 G CARBOHYDRATE

Tomato rolls with

a tasty pick-me-up that's practically fat-free

radishes

Serves 2:
4 wholemeal bread rolls
2 tbsp low-fat cream cheese
2 large tomatoes
4 radishes
1 small onion
small bunch chives
salt
black pepper

Slice the wholemeal rolls in two and thinly spread each half with the low-fat cream cheese. Wash and slice the tomatoes. Top and tail, wash, and slice the radishes. Peel and slice the onion. Arrange the onion rings on the bread roll halves with the sliced tomatoes and radishes.

Wash, shake dry, and snip the chives, then sprinkle them over the rolls. Season the rolls to taste with salt and pepper.

Wholemeal products

Wholemeal bread and rolls stay fresh for longer than their white-flour counter-parts. Stored in a lunch box with a tight-fitting lid, they will last for a good few hours without drying out and losing their flavour.

PER PORTION:

226 KCAL

11 G PROTEIN • 1 G FAT

43 G CARBOHYDRATE

power

Pear breakfast
zingy thanks to cranberries and pepper
slices

Serves 2: • 2 large dessert pears • 150 g (6 oz) cottage cheese • 4 tsp cranberry jelly • 4 slices wholemeal bread • black pepper

Halve, peel, core, and slice the pears. Combine the cottage cheese with half of the cranberry jelly. Spread the cottage cheese mixture over the slices of bread. Arrange the pear slices on top, season lightly with pepper, and garnish with the remaining cranberry jelly.

PER PORTION: 294 KCAL • 19 G PROTEIN • 5 G FAT • 46 G CARBOHYDRATE

Apple and mango
with coconut flakes and honey
muesli

Serves 2: • 10 tbsp jumbo rolled oats • 1 tbsp coconut flakes • 400 ml (14 fl oz) low-fat milk (1.5% fat) • 1 apple • 1 mango • honey to taste

Stir the rolled oats and coconut flakes into the milk. Wash, halve, peel, and core the apple, then cut into sticks. Cut the mango in half, remove the stone and peel, and cut into small pieces. Add the apple sticks and mango pieces to the flakes and combine thoroughly. Sweeten to taste with the honey.

PER PORTION: 256 KCAL • 7 G PROTEIN • 6 G FAT • 43 G CARBOHYDRATE

Marinated
a perfect packed lunch
vegetables

Wash, trim, and finely slice the celery. Wash, trim, and dice the courgette. Halve the red peppers, remove the stalk, seeds, and membranes, then wash, and dice finely. Transfer the sliced celery and diced courgette and pepper to a bowl, and season generously with salt and pepper.

Wash, trim, and finely slice the spring onions. Heat the olive oil in a frying pan. Brown the spring onions over a moderate heat. Add the passata or sieved tomatoes and leave over a low heat to thicken slightly.

Stir the tomato purée mixture into the vegetables and leave to stand in the bowl for at least 1 hour.

Wash the rosemary and use to garnish the vegetables. Serve with white bread.

Serves 2:

100 g (4 oz) celery
1 small courgette
2 large red peppers
salt
pepper
2 spring onions
1 tsp olive oil
100 ml (3 1/2 fl oz) passata/sieved tomatoes
1 small sprig rosemary
4 slices white bread

power

PER PORTION: 197 KCAL • 3 G PROTEIN • 6 G FAT • 33 G CARBOHYDRATE

Rocket salad with

with freshly grated Parmesan

melon

Serves 2: • 100 g (4 oz) rocket • 1 small galia melon • 2 tsp raspberry vinegar • 2 tsp lemon juice • salt • black pepper • 1 tsp olive oil • 20 g (1 oz) Parmesan

Wash the rocket, pick it over, removing any large stalks, and then chop. Halve the melon, remove the seeds, cut out the flesh, and chop into small pieces. Combine with the rocket. Mix together the raspberry vinegar, lemon juice, salt, pepper, and olive oil. Toss the rocket and melon pieces in the dressing and transfer to plates. Serve with a scattering of crumbled Parmesan.

PER PORTION: 163 KCAL • 7 G PROTEIN • 4 G FAT • 25 G CARBOHYDRATE

Italian spaghetti

delicious warm too

salad

Serves 2: • 80 g (3 oz) spaghetti • salt • 8 cherry tomatoes • 1 small courgette • 100 g (4 oz) mozzarella • 4 sprigs of basil • black pepper • 1 tsp apple vinegar

Cook the spaghetti in boiling salted water until *al dente*, then pour off the cooking water, refresh under cold water, and leave to drain. Wash and quarter the tomatoes. Wash, trim, and finely dice the courgette. Drain and finely dice the mozzarella. Wash the basil, shake it dry, and chop the leaves. Combine all the ingredients with the spaghetti and season to taste with the salt, pepper, and vinegar.

PER PORTION: 271 KCAL • 16 G PROTEIN • 9 G FAT • 33 G CARBOHYDRATE

Tex-Mex salad with
prepared in a jiffy
kidney beans

Serves 2: • 4 cherry tomatoes • 1 small onion • 3 tbsp kidney beans (tinned) • 100 g (4 oz) sweetcorn (tinned) • small bunch parsley • 2 tsp balsamic vinegar • salt • black pepper

Wash and quarter the cherry tomatoes. Peel, halve, and finely dice the onion, and combine with the tomato quarters, kidney beans, and sweetcorn. Wash the parsley, shake dry, then finely chop the leaves and add to the salad. Season to taste with the balsamic vinegar, salt, and pepper.

power

PER PORTION: 125 KCAL • 6 G PROTEIN • 1 G FAT • 23 G CARBOHYDRATE

Fruity
with apples and grapes
kohlrabi salad

Serves 2: • 1 medium kohlrabi • 2 apples • 100 g (4 oz) seedless grapes • juice of 1/2 lemon • juice of 1 orange • salt • black pepper

Peel and coarsely grate the kohlrabi. Wash, halve, core, and finely dice the apple. Wash the grapes thoroughly and cut in half. Combine the apple and grapes with the grated kohlrabi. Stir in the orange and lemon juice, and season to taste with salt and pepper.

power

PER PORTION: 130 KCAL • 2 G PROTEIN • 1 G FAT • 31 G CARBOHYDRATE

Turkey salad

rich in B-group vitamins for the nerves

with chicory

Wash the turkey breast and pat dry with kitchen paper. Heat the oil in a frying pan. Brown the turkey breast on both sides over a moderate heat

Serves 2:
150 g (6 oz) turkey breast
1 tsp vegetable oil
1 lemon
paprika
salt
black pepper
2 heads of chicory
2 oranges

for about 5 minutes. Squeeze the lemon, and combine the juice with a little paprika, salt, and pepper. Brush the marinade over the turkey breast and leave to cool for 10 minutes.

Meanwhile, trim, wash, and halve the chicory, remove the wedge-shaped stalks, and slice the lower part. Arrange the leaves of the upper part of the chicory on plates.

Peel the oranges, removing all the white pith. Remove the fruit from the orange segments, passing a small paring knife between the flesh and the membranes. Dice the turkey breast and combine with the orange segments and chicory slices. Season to taste with the paprika, salt, and pepper, and arrange on plates. For a packed lunch, put the salad in a plastic container with a tight-fitting lid.

power

PER PORTION: 175 KCAL • 21 G PROTEIN • 3 G FAT • 15 G CARBOHYDRATE

Sauerkraut with

not just for the digestion

pineapple

Serves 2: • 3 tbsp raisins • 100 g (4 oz) sauerkraut • 1 small pineapple • 2 tbsp apple juice

Soak the raisins in boiling hot water. Fluff up the sauerkraut with a fork. Quarter the pineapple

lengthways and remove the hard core. Remove the flesh from the skin and cut into small pieces.

Drain the raisins in a sieve and stir into the sauerkraut with the pineapple pieces. If the

sauerkraut is very dry, add the apple juice, and leave to stand for 1 hour.

PER PORTION: 208 KCAL • 2 G PROTEIN • 1 G FAT • 48 G CARBOHYDRATE

Quick chilled

with magnesium to combat stress

tomato soup

Serves 2: • 400 ml (14 fl oz) tomato juice • 200 ml (7 fl oz) vegetable stock • 2 dashes Tabasco • 1/2 tsp mild curry powder • salt • black pepper • grated zest of 1/2 unwaxed, or well scrubbed lemon • 4 basil leaves, finely chopped

Combine the tomato juice and vegetable stock, season with the Tabasco, curry powder, salt, and

pepper. Add the lemon zest to the soup, and chill in a refrigerator. To serve, sprinkle the soup

with the chopped basil.

PER PORTION: 167 KCAL • 18 G PROTEIN • 6 G FAT • 9 G CARBOHYDRATE

Fennel and
rich in iron and vitamin C
orange salad

Wash and trim the fennel, then cut in half lengthways. Cut the fennel halves into very thin slices. Peel one orange, removing all the white pith. Remove the fruit from the orange segments, passing a small paring knife between the flesh and the membranes. Peel, halve, and finely chop the shallot. Trim and wash the radicchio lettuce, shredding any large leaves.

Mix together the radicchio, sliced fennel, diced shallot, and orange segments. For the dressing, squeeze the remaining orange, and combine the juice with the mustard, vinegar, salt, and pepper. Stir in the oil. Toss the salad in the dressing and leave to stand for 20 minutes.

Serves 2:
1 fennel bulb
2 oranges
1 shallot
1/2 small radicchio lettuce
1 tsp mustard
1 tsp wine vinegar
salt
pepper
2 tsp walnut oil

Fennel

This popular, pale green bulb is a rich source of vitamin C, unrivalled even by kiwi fruit, oranges, or grapefruits. Fennel also contains more vitamin A than carrot juice or spinach. And it has almost as much calcium as full-fat milk, but with less than one tenth of the fat.

PER PORTION:

136 KCAL

6 G PROTEIN

4 G FAT

20 G CARBOHYDRATE

power

Fruity cheese
the sweet, vegetarian option
sandwich

Halve the bread rolls and thinly spread one half of each roll with butter. Wash and dry the lettuce leaves and arrange on the buttered halves. Wash the apple and peach thoroughly and halve them. Core the apple, and remove the peach stone. Finely dice the apple and peach halves. Stir the diced apple and peach into the low-fat cream cheese and spoon this mixture onto the lettuce leaves.

Peel the orange, removing all the white pith. Remove the fruit from the segments, passing a small paring knife between the flesh and the membranes. Add the orange segments to the fruit and cream cheese mixture and top with the remaining roll halves.

Serves 2:
2 long bread rolls
butter
a few lettuce leaves
(Lollo Biondo)
1 small apple
1 peach
5 tbsp low-fat cream cheese
1 orange

The freshness trick
To keep your sandwich crisp for hours and to prevent it from going stale, wrap it in several lettuce leaves and take it to work in a stay-fresh sandwich box.

PER PORTION:

343 KCAL

10 G PROTEIN • 5 G FAT

18 G CARBOHYDRATE

power

Sweet

for breakfast or elevenses

fruit rolls

Cut the rolls in half horizontally and spread each half with 1 tablespoon crème fraîche. Wash the tender, inside lettuce leaves, dry well, and place on the bottom halves of the bread rolls. Peel and slice the banana. Peel the orange, removing all the white pith. Remove the fruit from the segments, passing a small paring knife between the flesh and the membranes. Fold the sliced banana, orange segments, and raisins into the cream cheese, adding a little orange juice if necessary.

Spoon the mixture onto the lettuce leaves and top with the remaining bread roll halves.

Serves 2:
2 sesame wholemeal bread rolls
4 tbsp low-fat crème fraîche
4 inside lettuce leaves
1 banana
1 orange
1 tbsp raisins
3 tbsp low-fat cream cheese
(0.2% fat)
1 tsp orange juice (if necessary)

Low-fat crème fraîche

Instead of butter or margarine, you can use low-fat crème fraîche. It has only a quarter of the fat. You can also reduce the fat in recipes requiring crème fraîche by replacing half with low-fat crème fraîche.

power

PER PORTION:

263 KCAL

7 G PROTEIN • 8 G FAT

42 G CARBOHYDRATE

Bean sprout

hearty wholemeal snack with bean sprouts

sandwich with cheese

Serves 2: • 4 tbsp soya bean sprouts • 4 tbsp sour cream • mineral water • salt • pepper • 2 tomatoes • 4 slices wholemeal bread • 2 tsp tomato purée • 2 slices hard cheese (30% fat)

Wash the sprouts, combine with the sour cream, add a little mineral water, and beat until creamy. Season with salt and pepper. Wash and slice the tomatoes. Spread the slices of bread thinly with the tomato purée, spread the sprout mixture over two slices, then top with the tomatoes, cheese, and the remaining slices of bread.

PER PORTION: 329 KCAL • 18 G PROTEIN • 9 G FAT • 44 G CARBOHYDRATE

Red-and-green

a crispy, spicy snack to keep you going

baguettes

Serves 2: • 4 radishes • small bunch chives 02 small gherkins • 4 olives • 1/2 tsp mustard • 2 tbsp low-fat crème fraîche • 4 frisée lettuce leaves • 2 small baguettes • 2 tsp tomato purée

Trim and wash the radishes, then cut into small pieces. Wash and snip the chives. Cut the gherkins and olives into small pieces. Combine all of these with the mustard and low-fat crème fraîche. Wash the lettuce leaves. Cut the baguettes in half lengthways, and spread one half of each with the tomato purée. Place the lettuce leaves on top, then the crème fraîche mixture. Top with the remaining baguette halves.

PER PORTION: 238 KCAL • 7 G PROTEIN • 3 G FAT • 46 G CARBOHYDRATE

Sweet-and-savoury

lots of iron to give you plenty of energy

wholemeal sandwich

Serves 2:
6 slices of wholemeal toast
6 iceberg lettuce leaves
1/2 soft apple
1 tbsp cranberries
20 g (1 oz) low-fat liver sausage
60 g (3 oz) low-fat boiled ham

Lightly toast the wholemeal bread. Wash the iceberg lettuce leaves, shake dry, and remove the ribs from the leaves. Peel and core the apple, and crush with a fork. Combine with the cranberries and liver sausage.

Place two lettuce leaves each on two slices of wholemeal toast. Spread the liver sausage mixture thickly on top, cover each sandwich with a second slice of toast, and top with the ham and iceberg lettuce leaves. Top with the remaining slices of toast and cut the sandwiches in two diagonally.

> ## Light doesn't mean fat-free
>
> Many types of sausage and cheese also come in a light variety, so that you can cut down on fat in comparison with the full-fat version. However, always look at the total fat content. Because "light" doesn't mean "fat-free". Thus 100 g (4 oz) of "light salami" can still contain 24 g (1 oz) of fat.

PER PORTION:

406 KCAL

19 G PROTEIN • 11 G FAT

58 G CARBOHYDRATE

power

Spicy vegetable

full of minerals to get you fit

shake

Serves 2: • 12 radishes • 50 g (2 oz) broccoli • 200 ml (7 fl oz) tomato juice • black pepper • curry powder • 150 ml (5 fl oz) mineral water • 5 blades of chives

Trim and wash the radishes and broccoli, using only the small, outer rosettes of the broccoli. Purée the radishes and broccoli with the tomato juice, then pass through a sieve. Season with pepper and a little curry powder. Stir in the mineral water and pour into glasses. Wash and snip the chives. Sprinkle the chives and pepper over the drinks and serve.

PER PORTION: 30 KCAL • 2 G PROTEIN • 1 G FAT • 5 G CARBOHYDRATE

Pear and

a fresh, fruity pick-me-up

buttermilk flip

Serves 2: • 2 pears • 400 ml (14 fl oz) buttermilk • sugar • 1 tbsp coconut flakes

Peel, halve, and core the pears, then purée with the buttermilk. Sweeten to taste with a little sugar. Dissolve one teaspoon of sugar in a little water. Dip the rim of the glasses about 1 cm (1/2 in) into the sugared water, then into the coconut flakes. Pour in the drink, sprinkle with the remaining coconut flakes, and serve immediately.

PER DRINK: 146 KCAL • 4 G PROTEIN • 3 G FAT • 26 G CARBOHYDRATE

Banana power

magnesium and vitamin C to keep you fit

drink

Peel the bananas, cut off a few slices, and drizzle with 1 teaspoon of orange juice to prevent them from turning brown. Purée the remaining bananas, orange juice, and peanut butter using a hand-held blender. Slit the vanilla pods open lengthways, and scrape out the seeds with a knife. Stir them into the drink, and sweeten to taste with sugar. Pour the drink into two glasses.

Peel the orange, removing all the white pith. Remove the fruit from the segments, passing a small paring knife between the flesh and the membranes. Thread the orange segments and banana slices onto cocktail sticks and serve with the drink.

Serves 2:

2 bananas

400 ml (14 fl oz) orange juice

1 tsp peanut butter

2 vanilla pods

sugar

1 orange

Orange juice

Always make sure you buy 100 per cent fruit juices with no added sugar, and not fruit-flavoured drinks which may be only 50 per cent fruit juice, the rest being just sweetened water.

PER DRINK:

208 KCAL

3 G PROTEIN • 2 G FAT

41 G CARBOHYDRATE

White cabbage and
with red peppers on curried cabbage
cod parcels

Remove the outer leaves of the cabbage and carefully peel off 8 more leaves whole,

quickly blanching the whole cabbage beforehand if necessary. Cook the leaves in

boiling salted water for 12 minutes. Meanwhile, chop half of the

remaining white cabbage into small pieces, removing the core.

In a wide pan, bring the fish stock to the boil, add the cabbage,

and cook for 10 minutes. Halve the red peppers, remove the

stalks, seeds, and membranes, then wash and chop into small

pieces. Drain the large white cabbage leaves and lay them out

flat. Cut the cod fillet into four, place a piece of fish on one

white cabbage leaf, season with salt and pepper, and drizzle

with a little lemon juice. Place 1 tablespoon of chopped pepper

on each piece of fish. To make the parcels, wrap a second white

cabbage leaf around each portion of red pepper pieces and fish.

Serves 2:

1 small white cabbage (about 1.2 kg/2 1/2 lbs)

salt

400 ml (14 fl oz) fish stock (ready-made)

2 large red peppers (about 400 g/12 oz)

400 g (14 oz) cod fillet

white pepper

a few drops of lemon juice

curry powder or curry paste

2 tbsp chopped parsley

Add the remaining pieces of red pepper to the wide pan. Season to taste with

sufficient curry powder or 1 tablespoon curry paste, salt, pepper, and lemon juice to

make a spicy sauce. Place the white cabbage and cod parcels on top of the curried

cabbage and pepper mixture and cook for 8 minutes over a moderate heat. Spoon

the white cabbage and red pepper mixture onto plates and top with the parcels.

Serve with a sprinkling of parsley. Potatoes go very well with this dish.

power

PER PORTION: 297 KCAL • 43 G PROTEIN • 3 G FAT • 27 G CARBOHYDRATE

Fillet steak with

for the carnivores among us

broccoli rice

Strip the thyme and rosemary leaves from their stems. Wash the leaves, then chop finely, and stir into the oil in a bowl.

Serves 2:
1 sprig thyme
1 sprig rosemary
1 tsp vegetable oil
150 g (6 oz) fillet steak
75 g (3 oz) parboiled rice
150 ml (5fl oz) beef stock
(ready-made)
300 g (10 oz) broccoli
1 pinch nutmeg
salt
black pepper

Brush the fillet steak with the herb oil. Heat a non-stick frying pan. Brown the fillet steak on all sides over a moderate heat, then remove, wrap in kitchen foil, and keep warm. Lightly brown the rice in the same frying pan over a low heat, add the beef stock, and leave to soak for 15 minutes. Meanwhile, trim and wash the broccoli. Cut off the rosettes and add to the rice after about 5 minutes. Cook together with the rice for 10 minutes. Season the rice to taste with the nutmeg, salt, and pepper. Take the fillet steak out of the foil, cut in half, and arrange on plates with the broccoli rice. Serve immediately.

power

PER PORTION: 274 KCAL • 23 G PROTEIN • 5 G FAT • 33 G CARBOHYDRATE

Tuna and

packed with vitamin B2 for more energy

pasta bake

Boil the tagliatelle in salted water for 8–10 minutes until *al dente*. Preheat the oven to 180°C (350°F, Gas Mark 4). Peel and finely chop the onions. Heat the oil in a frying pan and soften the onions over a moderate heat. Wash, trim, and slice the mushrooms and add to the pan. Add the milk and boil over a moderate heat until it is reduced by half. Pour the tagliatelle into a sieve and leave to drain. Drain the tuna fish.

Finely chop the gherkins. Combine the tuna fish, gherkins, tagliatelle, and low-fat crème fraîche with the mushrooms, then season with salt and pepper. Transfer the mixture to a medium-sized casserole dish and bake on the middle shelf of the oven for about 20 minutes.

Serves 2:

100 g (4 oz) tagliatelle

salt

2 onions

1 tbsp olive oil

50 g (2 oz) mushrooms

100 ml (4 fl oz) low-fat milk (1.5% fat)

100 g (4 oz) tuna fish (tinned, in brine or spring water)

4 small pickled gherkins

2 tbsp low-fat crème fraîche

pepper

▶ **Light tuna fish**

Tuna fish not preserved in oil usually has less than 1 per cent fat, because it comes from lean pieces from a special type of tuna fish that is relatively low in fat. In contrast, fresh tuna fish from the fishmonger contains between 6 and 16 per cent fat.

power

PER PORTION:

316 KCAL

18 G PROTEIN • 8 G FAT

42 G CARBOHYDRATE

Vegetable

B-group vitamins to improve your mood and concentration

casserole with pork

Serves 2:
200 g (7 oz) lean pork
2 onions
1 small kohlrabi
250 g (8 oz) potatoes
1 tsp clarified butter
200 g (7 oz) frozen peas
400 ml (14 fl oz) vegetable stock
1 bunch parsley
1 pinch nutmeg
salt
black pepper

Cut the meat into large cubes. Peel and finely dice the onions. Peel and dice the kohlrabi and potatoes. Heat the clarified butter in a pan. Quickly brown the meat and onions over a moderate heat. Add the diced kohlrabi and potatoes to the meat, together with the frozen peas. Add the stock, and leave to simmer over a low heat for 20 minutes until tender. Meanwhile, wash the parsley, shake dry, strip the leaves from the stalks, and chop finely. Add the parsley to the stew and season to taste with the nutmeg, salt and pepper. Transfer to plates and serve.

Best reheated

Casseroles are perfect for preparing in advance and taking with you. They usually taste even better when reheated, because the flavours have developed over time. All you need to heat them up is an ordinary microwave oven.

PER PORTION:

554 KCAL

63 G PROTEIN • 16 G FAT

39 G CARBOHYDRATE

power

Celery and
orange rice

fresh, fruity, and satisfying

Serves 2: • 1 onion • 150 g (6 oz) celery • 1 tsp vegetable oil • 100 g (4 oz) brown rice • juice of 1 orange
• 2 tbsp raisins • nutmeg • salt • pepper

Peel and finely dice the onion. Wash, trim, and slice the celery. Heat the oil, then soften first the
onion, followed by the celery, over a moderate heat. Stir in the rice. Add the orange juice
together with 150 ml (5 fl oz) water. Add the raisins and simmer over a low heat for 30 minutes
or until the rice is cooked. Season with the nutmeg, salt and pepper. French bread goes well
with this dish.

PER PORTION: 253 KCAL • 6 G PROTEIN • 3 G FAT • 52 G CARBOHYDRATE

Potatoes with bean

rich in roughage and active substances

sprout cream

Serves 2: • 500 g (1 lb) waxy potatoes • 50 g (2 oz) mung bean sprouts • 2 tbsp sour cream • nutmeg
• salt • pepper • 3 tbsp sesame seeds

Boil the potatoes for about 25 minutes. Wash the mung bean sprouts and combine with the
sour cream, then season to taste with the nutmeg, salt, and pepper. Toast the sesame seeds in a
dry, non-stick frying pan until golden brown. Peel and halve the cooked potatoes, arrange them
on plates with the bean sprout and cream mixture, sprinkle with the toasted sesame seeds, and
serve with a green salad.

PER PORTION: 208 KCAL • 7 G PROTEIN • 6 G FAT • 32 G CARBOHYDRATE

Potato and
rich in roughage
celeriac bake

Preheat the oven to 200°C (400°F, Gas Mark 6). Meanwhile peel the potatoes and celeriac. Cut the potatoes into thick slices. Slice the celeriac very finely. Thoroughly wash and trim the leek, then slice the white and pale green part. Cut the ham into strips. Wash the parsley, shake dry, strip the leaves from the stalks, and chop.

Lightly grease a medium-sized casserole dish. Arrange the sliced potato and celeriac, the leek, then the ham in layers in the dish. Whisk together the vegetable stock, egg, and parsley, then season to taste with the nutmeg, salt, and pepper. Pour the mixture evenly over the casserole and bake on the middle shelf of the oven for about 30 minutes.

Serves 2:
3 floury potatoes
(about 500 g/1 lb)
1/2 small celeriac
1 leek
50 g (2 oz) lean boiled ham
1 bunch parsley
fat for greasing
150 ml (5 fl oz) vegetable stock
1 egg, 1 pinch nutmeg
salt
white pepper

Celeriac
When buying celeriac, check that it has a pleasantly sweet smell. The fresh, green celery leaf on the root indicates that the root is still crisp. And beware of a root that feels lighter than it looks: it could be woody inside.

PER PORTION:

220 KCAL

15 G PROTEIN

7 G FAT

24 G CARBOHYDRATE

power

Vegetable rice

packed with vitamins to make you fit

with Parmesan

Bring the vegetable stock to the boil in a pan. Add the brown rice and cook over a low heat for 30–40 minutes. Wash and trim the broccoli, then cut off the small rosettes. Halve the peppers, remove the stalks, seeds, and membranes, then wash and dice. After the rice has been cooking for 10 minutes, add the broccoli rosettes and the diced peppers, and cook for 20 minutes more. Grate the Parmesan and stir into the rice mixture. Season the vegetable rice to taste with the nutmeg, salt, and pepper. Wash the basil, shake dry, strip the leaves from the stalks, and chop coarsely. Transfer the vegetable rice onto plates and serve with a sprinkling of basil.

Serves 2:
200 ml (7fl oz) vegetable stock
100 g (4 oz) brown rice
150 g (6 oz) broccoli
1 large red and 1 large yellow pepper
50 g (2 oz) Parmesan
nutmeg
salt
black pepper
5 sprigs basil

43

► Tip

If you want to eat the vegetable rice at work, then don't sprinkle on the grated Parmesan and chopped basil until just before you are going to eat it. When reheated, the cheese makes the rice stick together, and the basil loses its flavour.

PER PORTION:

449 KCAL

34 G PROTEIN • 14 G FAT

47 G CARBOHYDRATE

power

Courgette and

a taste of the Orient with soy sauce, curry, and coriander

chicken soup

Carefully wash the chicken breast and cut it into small cubes. Combine the soy sauce and grape juice in a bowl. Add the diced chicken and marinate for about 30 minutes. Bring the chicken stock to the boil in a pan. Add the rice to the boiling chicken stock and cook for 10 minutes over a low heat.

Meanwhile, trim, peel, and chop the courgette. Add the chopped courgette to the stock, together with the chicken breast pieces and the marinade, and quickly bring to the boil, adding a little water to the soup if necessary. Season the chicken soup to taste with the curry powder, salt, and pepper. Serve the soup with a garnish of coriander leaves.

Serves 2:
100 g (4 oz) chicken breast
1 tsp soy sauce
2 tbsp grape juice
600 ml (1 pint) chicken stock
(ready-made)
50 g (2 oz) parboiled rice
1 courgette
curry powder
salt
black pepper
1 sprig coriander, washed

▶ It cooks itself

If you are making the soup in advance, then don't cook the rice, as it will become soft and mushy. The rice will cook itself as the dish is left to stand and then reheated.

power

PER PORTION:

167 KCAL

18 G PROTEIN • 3 G FAT

27 G CARBOHYDRATE

Beef with

a quick-fried feast

mushrooms

Serves 2:
150 g (6 oz) mushrooms
2 tsp lemon juice
1 tsp balsamic vinegar
100 ml (4 fl oz) meat stock
(ready-made)
iodized salt
pepper
150 g (6 oz) basmati rice
2 tsp olive oil
2 slices lean beef (weighing
about 150 g/(6 oz) each)
2 tsp freshly grated Parmesan

Trim the mushrooms, wipe with kitchen paper, and slice. Mix together the lemon juice, balsamic vinegar, beef stock, salt, and pepper. Add the sliced mushrooms and marinate for about 30 minutes. Preheat the oven to 200°C (400°F, Gas Mark 6). Bring about 300 ml (1/2 pint) salted water to the boil. Add the rice and cook over a low heat for about 15 minutes. Heat the oil in an ovenproof pan, and quickly fry the beef on both sides over a low heat, until it barely gives when pressed with the finger. Season with salt and pepper. Cover the meat with a thick layer of the sliced mushrooms. Sprinkle with Parmesan and bake on the middle shelf of the oven for about 5 minutes until golden brown. Serve with rice.

Beef

Together with fillet and roast beef, beef cuts from the rump, also called the thick flank or silverside, are particularly low in fat. To prevent the meat from becoming tough and dry when fried, choose meat that is marbled with fine threads of fat.

power

PER PORTION:

461 KCAL

39 G PROTEIN • 7 G FAT

58 G CARBOHYDRATE

Pasta with

an excellent source of iodine – to keep you fit

prawns

Serves 2: • 150 g (6 oz) pasta (made from durum wheat) • salt • 1 small onion • 2 tsp olive oil • 1 bunch basil • 4 tbsp sour cream • mustard • 150 g (6 oz) shelled prawns • pepper

Boil the pasta in salted water for 10 minutes until *al dente*. Peel and finely chop the onion. Heat the oil and gently fry the onion until it is translucent. Wash, shake dry, and chop the basil. Combine with the sour cream, a little mustard, and the prawns. Add to the onions, and season to taste with salt and pepper. Drain the pasta, toss in the onion mixture, and serve.

PER PORTION: 367 KCAL • 25 G PROTEIN • 8 G FAT • 55 G CARBOHYDRATE

Fennel gratin

serve with basmati rice

Serves 2: • 2 fennel bulbs • salt • 100 g (4 oz) smoked, rolled fillet of ham • small bunch parsley • 2 tsp lemon juice • 3 tbsp tomato purée • 50 g low-fat crème fraîche • pepper • 1 tbsp grated Parmesan

Trim and halve the fennel, then cook in salted water for 15 minutes until softened. Pour a little of the fennel cooking liquid into a shallow baking dish, then add the fennel. Preheat the oven to 200°C (400°F, Gas Mark 6). Chop the ham into small pieces. Wash and chop the parsley. Combine the ham, parsley, lemon juice, tomato purée, and crème fraîche, then season with salt and pepper. Spread this mixture over the fennel, sprinkle with the Parmesan, and bake in the middle of the oven for about 20 minutes.

PER PORTION: 223 KCAL • 25 G PROTEIN • 10 G FAT • 7 G CARBOHYDRATE

Oriental stir-fry

with fresh ginger and coconut milk

with pork fillet

Serves 2:
100 g (4 oz) basmati rice
iodized salt
200 ml (7 fl oz) meat stock
100 ml (4 fl oz) coconut milk
2 bananas
5 medium-sized carrots
3 spring onions
200 g (7 oz) pork fillet
2 tsp vegetable oil
50 g (2 oz) mung beans
a piece of ginger (walnut-sized)
small bunch parsley
pepper

Bring 200 ml (7 fl oz) salted water to the boil, add the rice, and cook over a low heat for 15 minutes. Meanwhile, bring the meat stock to the boil, stir in the coconut milk, and boil over a moderate heat until reduced by half. Peel the bananas, chop into small pieces, add to the stock, and bring back to the boil. Purée the coconut and banana sauce using a hand-held blender, and set aside.

Wash and peel the carrots and cut into strips. Wash and trim the spring onions, and cut into slices diagonally. Cut the pork fillet into strips. Heat the oil in a frying pan and fry the carrots and spring onions over a moderate heat for 3 minutes. Add the pork strips to the vegetables and cook over a low heat for 5 minutes until softened. Stir in the coconut and banana purée and simmer over a low heat for 15 minutes.

Wash and drain the mung beans and stir into the pork mixture. Peel and finely chop the ginger. Wash, shake dry, and finely chop the parsley. Season the vegetables with the ginger, salt, and pepper, then add the parsley. Arrange on plates with the basmati rice and serve.

power

PER PORTION: 474 KCAL • 31 G PROTEIN • 48 G FAT • 72 G CARBOHYDRATE

Tomato and
a variation on the popular original
mozzarella boats

Slice the top off each small baguette lengthways to form a lid. Remove the soft bread inside, and set the lids aside. Peel and finely chop the onion.

Serves 2:
4 small baguettes
1 onion
3 large tomatoes
1 tsp olive oil
150 ml (5 fl oz) vegetable stock
4 sprigs basil
100 g (4 oz) Mozzarella
salt
pepper

Wash the tomatoes, remove the stalks, and cut into pieces.

Heat the oil in a frying pan. Add the tomatoes, the bread from the inside of the baguettes, and the stock, and simmer over a low heat for about 5 minutes. Meanwhile, wash, shake dry, and finely chop the basil. Drain and dice the mozzarella.

Remove the frying pan from the heat and stir the basil and mozzarella into the tomato mixture.

Season with salt and pepper. Fill the hollowed-out baguettes with the tomato and mozzarella mixture and place the lid on top. Arrange the tomato and mozzarella boats on plates and serve immediately.

power

PER PORTION: 450 KCAL • 21 G PROTEIN • 9 G FAT • 70 G CARBOHYDRATE

Lambs' lettuce with
a light main meal – good for work too
trout fillet

Cook the potato for 25 minutes. Wash, trim, and thoroughly drain the lambs' lettuce. Peel and finely chop the onion and place in a bowl. Peel the cooked potato, then mash or crush it finely with a fork. Combine with the vegetable stock, vinegar, and olive oil. Season the dressing to taste with salt and pepper. Quickly heat the trout fillets through under a moderate grill or in a non-stick frying pan over a moderate heat, without adding any fat. Trim the mushrooms, wipe with kitchen paper, and slice finely.

Toss the lambs' lettuce in the dressing, arrange on plates, garnish with the sliced mushrooms, and serve with the warm trout fillets and the white bread.

Serves 2:
1 floury potato
100 g (4 oz) lambs' lettuce
1 small onion
5 tbsp vegetable stock (ready-made)
2 tbsp vinegar
1 tbsp olive oil
salt
pepper
2 smoked trout fillets
2 large mushrooms
4 slices white bread

Smoked trout

Trout fillets are hot-smoked at about 60°C (140°F). At this temperature, the fish retains its all-important unsaturated fatty acids. That is why smoked fish, whether trout, mackerel, herring, or salmon, is a healthy option. And another advantage for you is that, with a bread roll, they make an inexpensive but tasty work-time snack.

PER PORTION:

241 KCAL

14 G PROTEIN

7 G FAT

28 G CARBOHYDRATE

Polenta pizza with

simple sustenance to help the nerves cope with the stresses of everyday life

green pepper

Bring the vegetable stock to the boil, adding a little salt, then add the cornmeal. Return to the boil and cook over a low heat for at least 30 minutes, stirring constantly, until the dough lifts easily from the base of the pan. Grease a baking sheet. Shape the polenta dough into balls, then press out into rounds on the baking sheet to form small pizza bases. Preheat the oven to 200°C (400°F, Gas Mark 6). Combine the oil with the tomato purée. Wash the oregano, basil, and thyme. Shake dry, then strip the leaves from the stalks, and chop finely. Peel and crush the garlic, and stir into the tomato purée, together with the herbs. Season to taste with pepper. Spread the mixture out evenly over the polenta pizza bases.

Peel and finely chop the onion. Wash the tomatoes and cut into pieces. Halve the green pepper, remove the stalk, seeds, and membranes, then wash, and cut into small pieces. Scatter the onion and the chopped tomato and green pepper evenly over the polenta pizzas and sprinkle with the cheese. Bake the pizzas on the middle shelf of the oven for about 15 minutes until golden brown.

Serves 2:
500 ml (1 pint) vegetable stock
salt
100 g (4 oz) cornmeal
1 tbsp olive oil
2 tbsp tomato purée
1 sprig oregano
3 sprigs basil
2 sprigs thyme
1 clove garlic
black pepper
1 small onion
2 tomatoes
1 green pepper
2 tbsp grated Parmesan

power

PER PORTION: 321 KCAL • 12 G PROTEIN • 10 G FAT • 47 G CARBOHYDRATE

Fruit jelly

another way of serving fresh fruit

Soften the gelatine for 5 minutes in plenty of cold water. Peel and slice the banana. Wash, hull, and drain the berries. Peel the mandarin oranges and remove the fruit from the segments, passing a small paring knife between the flesh and the membranes. Bring the grape juice to the boil in a pan. Gently squeeze out the gelatine and dissolve in the grape juice. Stir in the sugar. Pour a thin layer of grape juice over the base of 2 single-portion jelly moulds or glasses. Place layers of fruit in the moulds or glasses and pour in the remaining grape juice. Leave the fruit jellies in the refrigerator for 4 hours to set.

To serve, loosen the jelly around the edges with a knife, stand the moulds for a few seconds in hot water, then turn out the jellies onto plates.

Serves 2:
4 gelatine leaves
1 banana
200 g (8 oz) seasonal berries
2 mandarin oranges
200 ml (7 fl oz) green grape juice
1 tbsp sugar

▶ Totally vegetarian

If you do not wish to use gelatine because it is made from animal bones, you can use agar-agar instead. It is made from seaweed and is available from health food stores. For this recipe, stir 1 level teaspoonful of agar-agar powder into 1 tablespoon of water. Then stir this into the boiling grape juice.

PER PORTION:

150 KCAL

5 G PROTEIN • 1 G FAT

31 G CARBOHYDRATE

Sweet millet risotto

the ideal combination – rich in iron and vitamin C

with mango

Bring the milk to the boil in a pan. Add the millet and cook over a low
heat for 20 minutes. Set the pan with the millet aside and leave to cool
for a few minutes. Then stir in the yogurt, honey,
and cinnamon.

Serves 2:

100 ml (4 fl oz) low-fat milk
(1.5% fat)

50 g (2 oz) millet

2 tbsp low-fat yogurt
(1.5% fat)

1 tsp honey

1 tsp ground cinnamon

1 mango

1 orange

1 tsp pistachio nuts

Cut the mango in half, remove the stone and peel,
and cut the flesh into small pieces. Peel the orange,
removing all the white pith. Remove the fruit from
the segments, passing a small paring knife between
the flesh and the membranes. Fold the mango pieces
and orange segments into the creamy mixture.

Transfer the millet risotto to dessert glasses, and
serve with a sprinkling of pistachio nuts.

Millet

This grain has twice as much iron as
rye or wheat and also contains more
magnesium than our traditional
varieties of corn. Just the right thing to
help you stand up to stress. If you
prefer your millet risotto not so grainy,
use a little more milk and cook it for
longer so that it swells up more.

PER PORTION:

205 KCAL

6 G PROTEIN

4 G FAT

37 G CARBOHYDRATE

power

Peach

with vanilla and honey cream cheese and almonds

gratin

Serves 2: • 100 g (4 oz) low-fat cream cheese • 1 tsp honey • 2 tsp vanilla sugar • 2 peaches • 2 tsp flaked almonds

Preheat the oven to 200°C (400°F, Gas Mark 6). Mix together the cream cheese, honey, and vanilla sugar. Wash and stone the peaches. Spoon the cream cheese mixture into the peach halves. Place the peach halves in two small, flameproof dishes, and bake on the middle shelf of the oven for 10 minutes. Toast the almonds in a dry, non-stick frying pan until golden brown, and sprinkle over the peaches. Serve warm.

PER PORTION: 122 KCAL • 8 G PROTEIN • 1 G FAT • 19 G CARBOHYDRATE

Grape and cream

a sweet source of energy – good as a main dish too

cheese soufflé

Serves 2: • 1 banana • 250 g (10 oz) low-fat cream cheese • 150 g (6 oz) green seedless grapes • 1 egg, separated • 2 tsp sugar • ground cinnamon • 1/2 tsp oil

Preheat the oven to 200°C (400°F, Gas Mark 6). Mash the banana, and stir it into the cream cheese. Wash the grapes, halve them and stir into the cream cheese with the egg yolk. Whisk the egg white into stiff peaks, adding the sugar and a little cinnamon. Fold the whisked egg white into the cream cheese mixture. Transfer the mixture to a small, greased soufflé dish and bake in the middle of the oven for 15 minutes.

PER PORTION: 232 KCAL • 21 G PROTEIN • 4 G FAT • 32 G CARBOHYDRATE

Polenta fruit loaf with
also makes a delicious cake
vanilla sauce

Serves 2:
100 g (4 oz) cornmeal
2 tbsp wheat flour
1 tbsp baking powder
salt
100 ml (4 fl oz) buttermilk
1 egg
1 tbsp honey
fat for greasing
200 g (8 oz) seasonal fruit
sugar
2 tsp cornflour
200 ml (7 fl oz) milk
1 vanilla pod

Preheat the oven to 200°C (400°F, Gas Mark 6). Combine the cornmeal, wheat flour, baking powder, and a little salt in a bowl. Add the buttermilk, egg, and honey, and mix thoroughly. Grease a small, shallow baking dish. Spoon the polenta mixture into the dish. Wash and hull the fruits, then chop them up into small pieces. Add sugar to taste if the fruits are sour. Spread the fruit pieces evenly over the polenta mixture. Bake the fruit loaf in the middle of the oven for about 20 minutes.

Meanwhile, combine the cornflour with 1 teaspoon of the milk in a small bowl. Bring the remaining milk to the boil, add the cornflour mixture, and bring back to the boil, stirring constantly. Slit the vanilla pod open lengthways, and using a knife scrape out the pulp into the milk. Sweeten the vanilla sauce to taste and serve with the polenta fruit loaf.

PER PORTION: 317 KCAL • 11 G PROTEIN • 5 G FAT • 57 G CARBOHYDRATE

Index

Low Fat recipes for home and away

First published in the UK by
Gaia Books Ltd, 20 High Street,
Stroud, GL5 1AZ
www.gaiabooks.co.uk

Registered at 66 Charlotte Street,
London, W1T 4QE
Originally published under the title
Low Fat

© Gräfe und Unzer Verlag GmbH
Munich. English translation copyright
© 2002 Gaia Books Ltd
Translated by Harriet Horsfield and edited by
E.M. Thomas in association with First Edition
Translations Ltd, Cambridge, UK
Typeset by The Write Idea in association with First
Edition Translations Ltd, Cambridge, UK

Editorial: Katherine Pate
Nutritional Advisor: Lorna Rhodes

Printed in Thailand

ISBN 1 85675 113 9
A catalogue record for this book is available in
the British Library

10 9 8 7 6 5 4 3 2 1

Caution
The techniques and recipes in this book are to be used at
the reader's sole discretion and risk. Always consult a
doctor before beginning a new eating plan or if in doubt
about a medical condition.

Friedrich Bohlmann is a nutritional scientist and
nutrition consultant. He has been a journalist for many
years, writing for major German newspapers. He is the
nutrition expert for the German daily television
programme "Leben und Wohnen" (Living life to the full).
He has written several guide books and was awarded the
German Nutrition Society's journalists' prize.

Susie M. and **Pete Eising** have studios in Munich
(Germany) and Kennebunkport, Maine (USA). They
studied at the Munich Academy of Photography, where in
1991 they set up their own studio for food photography.

For this book:
Photographic design:
Martina Görlach
Food styling:
Monika Schuster

Thanks to the following for their help with photographic
production:
Le Creuset (Notzingen, Germany)
Sabre (Paris)
Designer Guild (Germany)
LSA (London)

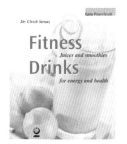

BRAIN FOOD
Food to increase mental agility
Dr Ulrich Strunz
£5.99
ISBN 1 85675 197 X
Food to stimulate your brain.
Increase your IQ, improve
your memory and speed up
your thought processes.

FITNESS DRINKS
Juices and smoothies for energy
and health
Dr Ulrich Strunz
£5.99
ISBN 1 85675 103 1
Delicious recipes for protein-
packed power drinks rich in
essential vitamins and
minerals.

FITNESS FOOD
Recipes to increase energy,
stamina and endurance
Doris Muliar
£5.99
ISBN 1 85675 167 8
No more lethargy and
exhaustion. Healthy food for
power, conditioning and
performance during exercise
and afterwards.

FAT BURNER
Eat yourself slim
Marion Grillparzer and
Martina Kittler
£5.99
ISBN 1 85675 108 2
How to eat well and lose
weight. Delicious foods that
burn away excess fat and
make you feel fantastic.

ENERGY DRINKS
Power-packed juices, mixed,
shaken or stirred
Friedrich Bohlmann
£5.99
ISBN 1 85675 140 6
Fresh juices packed full of
goodness for vitality and
health.

ANTI STRESS
Recipes for acid-alkaline balance
Dagmar von Cramm
£4.99
ISBN 1 85675 155 4
A balanced diet to reduce
stress levels, maximise
immunity and help you
keep fit.

DETOX
Foods to cleanse and purify
from within
Angelika Ilies
£5.99
ISBN 1 85675 150 3
Detoxify your body as part of
your daily routine by eating
nutritional foods that have
cleansing properties.

LOW CHOLESTEROL – LOW FAT
The easy way to reduce
cholesterol, stay slim and
enjoy your food
Döpp, Willrich and Rebbe
£4.99
ISBN 1 85675 166 X
Stay fit, slim and healthy
with easy-to-prepare
gourmet feasts.

To order the books featured on this page call 01453 752985, fax 01453 752987 with your credit/debit card details, or
send a cheque made payable to Gaia Books to Gaia Books Ltd., 20 High Street, Stroud, Glos., GL5 1AZ.
e-mail: gaiapub@dircon.co.uk or visit our website www.gaiabooks.co.uk